R.J. Tolson Page-Turners & Upcoming Works

The Chaos Chronicles Series

Book 1:
Zephyr the West Wind: Final Edition

Book 2:
Hugh the Southern Flame

The Project: Limitless Series

Volume 1:
The Success Initiative

Other Releases:

Blood Red Love

Sage Endeavors: A Collection of Short Stories

Deep Truths: A Collection of Poetry

The Lost Chronicles of Rave

For previews of upcoming books by R.J. Tolson and more information about the author, visit: www.rjtolson.com.

Praise for Project: Limitless Volume 1, The Success Initiative and R.J. Tolson

"If you could read only one book this year, you have it in your hands."
Akihiro Sato, manga artist and judo business founder

"To do more, have more, and be more... read, absorb, and apply this wonderful book. It's a winner—and you will be too!"
Tatiana Shabelnik, fashion designer and founder of Belorusochka Couture

"Warning: The content of this book is highly contagious. Even slight exposure may set you on a path to broadening your horizons, a radical reboot of your priorities, deep contentment, and, of course, success."
Mark Janson, CIO of Basketball Sports High and philanthropist

"Once in a generation, a book comes along that can truly transform your life. This is it. Project: Limitless doesn't show you just how to start becoming more successful; it shows you how to realize and experience what matters most."
Anjeza Angie Gega, singer, actress, author, dancer, model, humanitarian

"Let this book jump-start you, guide and propel you into your future. You will be on the fast track for reaching your goals and achieving the success you desire in no time. Read it and reread it. It will work for you!"
Jordan Swain, editor-in-chief and publisher of *Vanichi Magazine*, motivational speaker

Project: Limitless Volume 1: The Success Initiative

R.J. Tolson

This edition first published in 2014

© 2014 R.J. Tolson

RJTIO/Universal Kingdom Print
Published by Universal Kingdom Print
United States of America
10 9 8 7 6 5 4 3 2 1

For details on our global editorial offices, customer service, and information about applying for permission to reuse the copyright material in this book, see our website at www.universalkingdominternational.com.

All rights reserved. No part of this book may be reproduced, scanned, or distributed in any printed or electronic form without permission. Please do not participate in or encourage piracy of copyright materials in violation of the author's rights. Purchase only authorized editions.

Designations used by companies to distinguish their products are often claimed as trademarks. All brand names and product names used in this book are trade names, service marks, trademarks, or registered trademarks of their respective owners. The publisher is not associated with any product or vendor mentioned in this book. This publication is designed to provide accurate and authoritative information regarding the subject matter covered. It is sold on the understanding that the publisher is not engaged in rendering professional services. If professional advice or other expert assistance is required, the services of a competent professional should be sought.

While the author has made every effort to provide accurate telephone numbers and Internet addresses at the time of publication, neither the publisher nor the author assumes any responsibility for errors or for changes that occur after publication. The publisher does not have any control over and does not assume any responsibility for author or third-party websites or their content.

Many Universal Kingdom Print books are available at special quantity discounts for bulk purchase for sales promotions, premiums, fundraising, and educational needs. For details, contact the author, author's official representative, or publisher.

Project: Limitless Logo Design by Nolan Kabrich
Logo © 2014 R.J. Tolson

ISBN-13: 978-0990329909
ISBN: 0990329909
Universal Kingdom Print

Dedication

This book is dedicated to my grandfather, who has given me the opportunity for an education from the best institutions, support throughout my life, and the wisest, most philosophical, most meaningful advice I could wish for. I never would have gotten into the business world without him.

Hey, look—I couldn't leave you with that slight fleeting emotion feeling of picking up a book and finding that the dedication isn't to you. Well, this time it's different. To all the readers, whether we have met, haven't, may in the future, or never will—this one's for you.

Acknowledgements

I wish to thank, first and foremost, my parents and my grandparents for, well, everything. I wouldn't be here today without them.

I would also like to thank:

Glenn and Cecilia Woods, Lee and Deborah Woods, Mark and Susan Woods, and Strick and Lisa Woods, for all their support throughout my entire life. And for the last few years, I have had Charles Monzeglio and Koop Sel to thank for this too.

My editor, Stephanie Mitchell, who is just absolutely brilliant and provided insightful feedback to help with polishing efforts.

All of the RJTIO staff and volunteers for their feedback and enthusiastic support. Julie and Angie both offered great advice! Nolan Kabrich's designs and effort at making my life easier while writing this were invaluable.

My best friends, with their unflagging support for my expanding list of projects, enterprises, and passions.

My younger first cousins, William, Vanessa, Collin, Brooke, and Samantha, along with my niece, Meghan, who inspire me to make the world a better place for them to live in.

And finally, and most importantly, cheers to you who picked up this book. Your pursuit of success only shows that the human Will of Fire is burning strong and will continue to do so in the future. I hope that you will let me know how your life adventure develops (www.facebook.com/authorrjtolson).

Contents

Part One

1	**The Universe and You**	**3**
	The Keys to Success	3
	Self-Identification	5
	Pandora's Box	10
	Your Destiny	13
2	**Origins**	**14**
	Historical Legacy	15
	The Beginning of Change	15
	Your Legacy	16
3	**Doctor Who?**	**20**
	The Power in Knowledge	20
	Broadening Your Horizons	21
	The Unspoken Advantage	24
4	**Anti-Procrastination**	**26**
	The Zone	26
	Strength in Habits	27
	Mental Attitude	28
	Inspiring Environment	30
	M. D. O.	31

Part Two

5	**The Question**	**36**
	Questioning Your World	36
6	**The Muses**	**39**
	The Musemobile	39
7	**Imagination**	**41**
	Stigma	41
	The First Wave	42
8	**Enlightenment**	**43**
	Evaluation	43
	Parameters	44
	Guided Imagination	45
9	**Innovation**	**46**
	The Forged Path	46
	The Abyss of Fear	48
	Alibis	49
	Packing Up	49
10	**The Will of Fire**	**50**
	Lighting the Torch	50

About R.J. Tolson   **52**

PART ONE

Chapter 1:
The Universe and You

People who want to make positive change, whether on a personal level, a community level, or even a global level affecting humanity, all start at the same place: the path to success. Successful people share many common qualities in both their personal and business lives, all of which stem from the recognition and use of the ultimate tool every human has at their disposal—their BRAIN. The result: a massive step toward relative self-enlightenment, the ability to achieve their goals and dreams, and limitless personal power that can lead to true bliss. But if we all have this tool, why do only a few succeed while so many fail?

As the world has changed, and the structure of society along with it, people in recent years have been fed a detrimental lie. Sixty years ago, studying hard in school, getting a top-notch college degree, and maybe even completing some form of grad school guaranteed success (and happiness). Today, as many hard-working graduates have seen, that is no longer true.

Power is in the eye of the beholder. If you wish to succeed, especially in today's world, you must recognize that everything—anything around you—can be made into an opportunity. But to utilize such opportunities, you must educate yourself in real-world skills, broaden your horizons through diversity of knowledge, capabilities, and mindsets that will get you ahead of the competition. The challenge is fierce. The path ahead will be worth the effort, but not easy. Luckily enough, from the moment your life force entered into this world, you were born not just to reach ahead, but to achieve success. This book is meant to help guide you on your path.

The Keys to Success

Since the beginning of humanity, success in any field has required, at the very least, three strong qualities at heart: an open mindset, an undying will, and the ability to innovate. These three qualities have separated the successful from the failed time and time again, and today is no different.

An Open Mind
The phrase "an open mind" has many meanings and connotations. In this book, I use it to mean having the sense to know when to talk and when to listen, as well as not merely accepting but welcoming the unfamiliar, the different, and the new. This includes trying to take in and understand other opinions, for whether you agree or disagree, trying to understand is the goal. Recognizing the strands of reality leaves us with gardens of possibilities, and there are many ways to grow and cultivate them.

But being open-minded can be tough sometimes. Most people have strong views about specific topics and find it hard to hear other perspectives, let alone be swayed from their own opinions. Of course, having strong beliefs does not have to mean having a closed mind. For many, such beliefs give reason to live, to move forward, and to act—many times, this is a good thing. Though it can truly be tough sometimes—even for some of the most successful people in life—I've always found I have reaped far more benefits being open-minded than not, and I know I would not have been able to succeed without such a mindset.

A Strong Will
Are you not easily daunted or discouraged? Do you hold firm convictions? Do you often refuse to accept defeat? Are you fiercely loyal? Determined to succeed? Extraordinarily devoted to accomplishing your goal(s)? If so, you happen to be a strong-willed person. If not, or you can say yes to just a few of these questions, that is okay!

In reality, most people aren't strong-willed, or at least can't easily express the fact that they are. Fortunately, although there are many factors that contribute to a weaker or stronger will, we all have a torch and flame within us. A weaker flame represents potential for growth, while a strong, burning flame represents a strong, steady will. This is referred to as the Will of Fire, and just as one torch can light another, strong-willed people can spread inspiration to others as well.

Having a strong will is one of the foundational building blocks on the path to success. It can help a person persevere in the face of adversity, to never give up, and to set and pursue goals. You may have a strong will naturally, you may have nurtured one over time, or you may need to develop your flame by drawing upon sources of strength and inspiration to achieve your goals. No matter where you're standing, continuous growth and development are essential for a successful and happy life. Below is a list of a few things that become easier as your will strengthens:

- To speak up for what's right
- To practice and improve a skill
- To achieve excellence
- To overcome adversity
- To maintain consistent effort
- To be patient
- To be loyal
- To oppose what's wrong
- To defend or protect self-interest

- To express personal opinions
- To be hardworking
- To set and pursue goals

The Ability to Innovate

The caveman's fire. The wheel, the bicycle. The automobile. The computer, Internet, smartphone, tablet. What do all of these have in common, at their very base? They were all innovations. The most common definitions for "innovation" include "a new idea, method, or device" and "an improvement to something already existing." But what does this really mean?

I want you to think of the world as a bunch of particles lumped together to make what you see today—your reality. Many people believe that the established, visible particles they see every day are the only ones in existence, all there are. As such, their lives go along according to these known particles, and so choices and solutions are based on them, as well as many conclusions. Many companies, organizations, and people build their entire businesses or lives on these particles, trapping themselves in what is known as the status quo—life or business as usual.

Eventually, someone comes along and sees particles beyond the common ones of every day—particles that are ignored, missed, or not visible to those not open to them. These newcomers are visionaries or innovators. What is the source of their insight? Unexpected or new connections between particles, ideas, notions, possibilities, and of course the imagination. Many of today's common particles were once uncommon, innovations, like the laptop computer. So what is innovation but the ability to see these uncommon particles and produce upon on them?

Being an innovator means not only having such a skill but also knowing that the particles you see are a) rational and b) mandatory for humanity and for the world to move forward.

Self-Identification

At this stage, a logical and very important question would be what all this has to do with you as you are now, and how you can utilize such information. But then again, to understand the answers, a core question must be brought to light: who are you?

Exercise
Ask yourself the question "Who Am I?" and record your response below:

How did you answer the question? Most often, our answers come from things we associate ourselves with rather than our true essence—and this is a common problem. What I mean by "associated things" are answers like "I am a soccer player," "I am twenty-one years old," "I am a son," or "I am from Los Angeles." But these external situational concepts are not who you are, and by allowing your identity to be defined by people or things outside of you, you become dependent on those external things. How can you expect to become successful in a world where you must interact with and influence/be influenced by others if you don't first know who you truly are?

The answer to the question "Who am I?" cannot be found in your past or by external means. The most natural response to the above exercise is to list accomplishments, relations, self-stats, or interests—and answering that way isn't wrong. But to truly know who you are, you must detach yourself from these external concepts. The fact is, you have known who you are since the day you were born, long before the life you have experienced and witnessed had clouded your perspective. Living in a society that praises "doing" rather than "inner findings" has left many people confused. But what does a truthful insight look like?

Start by thinking of an activity that you absolutely love doing, that makes you love who you are when you are doing it, and that when you are involved in it, you lose track of time and feel like it is really you. It can be something like running on the beach or playing basketball or even shopping. My own example: I love writing and coming up with new plots. Time flies by; I know I am completely into it and present. When I am writing, I am pensive, creative, clearly focused, passionate, energetic, philosophical, and innovative. Those qualities are a reflection of who I am, and my answer to "Who am I?" is "I am pensive, creative, focused, passionate, energetic, philosophical, and innovative." Below, follow the exercise and write down your own personal example.

Exercise

Take your own list of qualities and create your own "I am" statements. Read them aloud every day, even if only for a quick moment to remind yourself of who you are.

So now that you can answer the question "Who am I?", you must understand the way you look at yourself and your relationship to the world. Four players define your relationship to the world: identity, self-esteem, boundaries, and the ideal self.

Identity
The global understanding you have of yourself is your identity. Self-identity stems from self-assessments, for example of your skills and abilities, occupation, hobbies, or personality and physical attributes. Your most recent answer to "Who am I?" belongs in this category, as it explains your very specific present self. But self-identity includes both your past and present selves. We'll explore this in the ideal-self category.

Self-Esteem
Our overall evaluation of our own worth at any one point in time constitutes our self-esteem. This aspect of our person is probably the most important emotional gauge of our ability to feel other positive emotions and hold positive beliefs about ourselves. This is vital, because it affects what we see and measure as success, confidence, security, and happiness.

As a general state of mind, self-esteem is affected by changes in any one of the feelings that make it up. A drop in security creates a short-term negative effect, while positive events like success on a project create positive sensations.

Boundaries and Worldview
These concepts influence your self-esteem directly. But what is a boundary, and what are worldviews in this context? Your boundary is a clear and defined border that surrounds your self. Think of a castle as the boundary and the king or queen inside as the (your) self. The boundary lines, or castle walls, let you and others know what you will accept in behavior toward and from you and define your capability to say either yes or no to events or statements. As an example, imagine you sometimes hang out with someone who may do something on a small illegal scale once in a while. They push you to join them while you are together. Are you comfortable saying no?

Our worldview is the structure that we utilize to define what the world is. The worldview looks at the question "Who are we?" rather than "Who am I?" by including the physical and meta-universal life, culture, and society. This is what allows us to create a standard of how we think things are and should be. It defines our morals, our rules of life, and how we relate and conduct ourselves within the world. Each and every worldview is relative; we create it through our experiences, intellect, and the decisions we make. Our worldview and boundaries are the filters through which we judge ourselves and others—when you experience an event that supports your worldview, your self-esteem increases; when you experience an event that counters your worldview, your self-esteem decreases.

The Ideal Self
This is simply how you wish you could be. In many cases, the way our worldview and boundaries are constructed define our ideal-self image, and our self-esteem is measured according to how much we are like our ideal selves in a general sense. This concept of our future selves or possible selves represents our theories of what we would like to become, and also what we fear becoming. The future or ideal self is our evaluative contrast to our current self. It can provide inspiration for our future behavior.

In summary, identity, boundary/worldview, self-esteem, and the ideal self are the building blocks of the self, or who you are on a personal and global scale. Your identity (the core of who you are) is guarded by your boundary, which filters experiences based on your worldview, defines your ideal self, and allows you to measure up to it through self-esteem. Here is a metaphorical example: a king of a kingdom is the core, his castle is a boundary which only lets in whom he wishes (worldview), the ideal self is Camelot (the perfect kingdom), and self-esteem is determined by how well the king thinks his kingdom measures up to Camelot.

Understanding who you truly are and being able to answer "Who am I?" properly gives you many important advantages on the path to success and a rewarding life. This process is similar to wisdom. You are building your character, which creates control, filters what is acceptable, and determines when you do things. Below are benefits that come from knowing who you are.

1. **Decision-making is easier and more spot on**. By knowing and being who you are, you see with the wisdom of hindsight in foresight—you only struggled with decisions in the past because you were choosing from options that did not fit you, dictated by society.

2. **Hidden wisdom is more accessible**. Use the key, questioning your most challenging self-discoveries, for within those questions and answers are connections and realizations that form powerful insights.

3. **Productiveness comes with less effort**. Authenticity allows access to a part of you not unveiled before, a part that calls for willpower, discipline, and self-control to get things done.

4. **Uncovered opportunities are seen through a new lens**. Once you know who you are, you can see more paths, and specifically the opportunities they present and fit to you.

5. **Your dreams, not those crafted by elements around you, become visible**. The desire of your heart of hearts feeds into true happiness and allows you to feel true passion and recognition of the gifts you possess.

6. **You can create aligned work.** This work is your natural edge in the world, work that is your calling, work that will allow you to achieve fulfillment and reap rewards.

Pandora's Box

If you want to achieve success, you must understand something—something that has nothing to do with your talents, education, or financial status. **You must understand that if you want success, you need to know what you're willing to sacrifice to achieve it.** It is always easy and fun to talk the talk about what you want to do, to achieve, but by asking yourself one question, you can test the authenticity of your claim—**how much are you willing to give up for it?**

Exercise
Below is space for you to write what you think you should, will, and can give up to achieve success. Some of my past sacrifices include TV, self-doubt, video games, soccer, and candy.

The truth is, most people just talk the talk. Ask any level of entrepreneur if they want to succeed, and no doubt you will hear a clear **YES**. Include the average person, and you'll get responses like "I don't think I can win, but I'll make it far," or "I don't think I'll be a billionaire, but I'll make a ton of money." But ask these people what they are willing to sacrifice, suffer, or tolerate to achieve, and you'll get answers that show you most people subconsciously know they don't have what it takes—they won't give it their all, and some even expect success to be instant and effortless.

In Greek mythology, Pandora was a woman given the task of watching over a container—which she was told never to open. Unable to control her curiosity, Pandora opened the container and let out all the evils of the world (greed, despair, hatred). Distraught at what she had done and fearing the wrath of Zeus, she quickly tried to close the container, only to find hope at the bottom.

In this case, Pandora's box represents what may be on the path ahead. The evils represent the harsh thorns that may block the path and make us sacrifice convenience and comfort to retrieve our prize. In humanity's case, as in Pandora's, there remains hope—in yours case, this is your dream. A very small minority are able and willing to give it their all from the get-go. They don't accept or recognize any limits—and they don't settle for anything less than their grand goals. You may be thinking, "To achieve success, why do I have to give up something?" To truly be committed to a desire, a goal, you must be willing to sacrifice for it.

What do you have to give up? Only you can decide, in the long run. You will find, though, that giving up past ways of thinking and not having a closed mind are among the first. Think of what you sacrifice as an investment—a temporary loss that will only contribute to long-term success! Recognizing your strength and being able to sacrifice only helps you. The key is deciding to commit and take that first step.

Exercise
Below, answer the question "What are you willing to give up to achieve success?" again. Don't hold back!

Your Destiny

The universe is filled with opportunities—but only you can decide to take them. You control the building blocks of your destiny. Not only does this mean that you define the outcome of your life and the fulfillment of your dreams, but also that you have limitless potential. To be successful will require you to take control of your potential, to harness it, and to achieve. For some, such a process may come easily. For many, it doesn't. But all of us hold one thing in common at our very cores—limitless potential, and the option to push through and achieve success.

Your destiny is yours to define. Your desire is your fuel. Your truth and knowledge are your power. Now continue forward with an open mind—your future of success awaits.

Chapter 2:
Origins

The past, present, and future all play important roles on any path to success. But unlike the future and present, the past has already occurred, giving us an advantage that many overlook due to ignorance. Why is the past, the origin of revolutionary success and chance, important to you on your journey to your own success?

      History is important because it guides our actions in the present. Essentially, WE ARE THE PAST: the sums of all events, positive, negative, and indifferent, that have occurred throughout time. This applies to the societal and global levels as well as the individual level. Understanding not only the end result but also the way it came to be has far-reaching importance. If we don't understand what made someone the way they are, we often make many mistakes in our interactions with them. Think about how you treat someone based on what you know of him or her. This extends to interactions between countries on the international level and businesses on the industry level (culture and experience define marketing projections).

      History is our guide for the present, helping us understand and improve upon both our mistakes and our triumphs so that we can shape a better future.

1. **Global judgment:** History is our biggest pool of evidence for why people behave the way they do.
2. **Critical thinking skills:** Studying history promotes reading at an advanced level (evaluation, synthesis, analysis).
3. **Social diversity:** Solutions to problems, especially difficult or pervasive ones, require insights formed by diverse experiences and perspectives.
4. **Inspiration and legacy:** History has taught us that, whether positively or negatively, one man or woman can succeed and truly change the world—Mohandas Gandhi, Alexander the Great, Mother Teresa, Steve Jobs, Martin Luther King, and Queen Elizabeth are only a few. It also shows us that what you do now has the power to extend far beyond one lifetime.

Historical Legacy

Each individual, whether a king or queen of old, a civil revolutionary, or a janitor, forms a unique legacy. Actions that have shaped the structure of the animal kingdom, formed a perspective on physical attributes, or even left a beautiful cake for sale in a bakery—all have one aspect in common: they are reminders of what humans have done, and of our limitless potential as individuals and as a whole. For you, those legacies should not only be a place to draw inspiration from but a place to expand your knowledge, learn how to think outside the box, and improve on.

The Beginning of Change

There is no definitive moment marking the beginning of individual human success, but a good place to start is with one known to have first enacted the spark of change that influences how we think of success. Overlooked by many, Anaximander is the first philosopher to have written down his ideas. The pre-Socratic ancient Greek philosopher began to think out side of the box for his time—he tried to define elements of the universe surrounding him. Not so long after, Confucius, Socrates, Aristotle, and Plato followed. They were successful, not in an industrial sense, but in a tremendous revolutionary one—their actions and achievements have shaped the present and thus the future.

Take Augustine of Hippo for example. He is known as the father of Christian philosophy for his great piece of literature, *Confessions*. René Descartes, a French philosopher of the sixteenth century, established what became known as the "method of doubt," a way to establish a basis of "certain knowledge." The number of legacies to pull inspiration from for your success is unfathomable. Some of them include the printing press, a dream achieved by Johannes Gutenberg; the electric light, first pioneered by Sir Humphry Davy (inventor of the carbon ore lamp) and later popularized by Thomas Alva Edison; and Alexander Fleming's success in discovering penicillin in 1928. More recently, success has continued in new and different areas of life.

At age forty-six, J. K. Rowling is estimated to have a fortune of $1 billion. As of 2011, she had sold over 450 million books, and the Harry Potter series has been translated into over sixty-seven languages. But in 1990, when it all began for her, Rowling was at a very different place in life. Her mother had just passed away, she had to ask the state for assistance to provide for herself and her daughter, and she was working as a researcher. But what does her eventual success mean to you?

It doesn't matter what your craft is, you can find a way to be successful.

Never give up, especially when it starts to get tough. The light may just be around the corner.

Adopted into a lower-middle-class family in the 1950s, Steve Jobs grew up in Santa Clara County, California. Years later, Jobs enrolled at Reed College, dropping out after one semester to digress into diets, philosophy, and the infamous LSD. After working for Atari, Jobs travelled to India, later returning to join a friend in their shared interest in electronics. The rest is history. Eventually he founded Apple, and after many events, he returned as CEO and revolutionized the world with the iPod and related products. Before his passing, Steve Jobs had a net worth of $10.2 billion. There are many lessons to take from his legacy, including:

1. Stick firmly to your vision and goal.
2. Understand the limits of your power.
3. Loyal employees are important; treat others the way you wish to be treated.
4. Never fear failure.
5. No matter how much you plan, there are always unpredictable elements. Don't look at them as a negative, but a positive. They may sow the seeds of your future success.
6. Expect a lot from yourself—and others.
7. Find the most talented people to surround yourself with. Apple wasn't just Steve Jobs, but everyone in the company who did their part.

With unlimited legacies to choose from, I choose two very different modern people who not only inspired me personally but revolutionized the world through the achievement of their success. No matter your goal or dream, previous generations have attempted to achieve in similar ways—their history is your advantage. Learn not only to inspire yourself, but to challenge the status quo by making your own dream come true.

Your Legacy

When I was seventeen years old and still just a senior in high school, something inside me clicked. It wasn't a sudden burst of drive or inspiration, or the occurrence of an external life-altering event. I hadn't lost an arm, or been contracted by Zeus to embark on a great quest, like those depicted in mythology. Instead, it was quite simple; I realized that I wanted to do something great—and I had to succeed at any cost.

Origins

I didn't graduate high school as valedictorian, a prized athlete, or every teacher's favorite—all of which are great accomplishments. I did, however, complete and publish a full-length fantasy novel, found a web design company, speak six languages, and create a positive life change. At eighteen, a freshman in college, I had expanded my company so that it was large enough to contract thirty employees while hosting three separate divisions, including the charitable Forever Trust. By the time I was nineteen, my parent company contracted around sixty employees, having now expanded into four different industries through its divisions. I had also published two books, started a national literary campaign, and sunk my teeth into metaphysics.

In my twentieth year, I contracted over a hundred employees and thousands of Forever Trust volunteers; became an award-winning author, internationally recognized CEO, and inspirational speaker; and traveled across the globe inspiring others to make their dreams come true. I didn't have rich parents funding my every move, a wealth of experience and knowledge, or even a high school degree when I started out. Instead, I was lucky enough to have a supportive family—along with the library, the Internet, a specific skill set, and an experienced and wise mind to pitch my ideas to.

Aside from my less and less special everyday coming-of-age story, what does it mean for you? Well, it gives you a close-up and personal origin legacy to take advantage of as you begin to pave your own. You don't have to be a billionaire author or tech genius to make a difference. I remember my grandmother's funeral like it was yesterday; at it, neighbors, friends, coworkers, peers, and relatives spoke about how warm and compassionate she was, how she was strong, not for just having raised her five children with my grandfather, but for how in her own life she had lived for what she believed in. A seamstress for Billie Holiday, mother, grandmother, friend, and civil rights activist, she helped changed the world one step at a time in her own way. That was her legacy—how she touched other people's lives.

The Success Initiative

Exercise
In the space below, answer, "What will your legacy be?"

On that particular day, in the seventeenth year of my life, I sat on the field where I had just played my last varsity high school soccer game ever. Nostalgic, I looked across it at the other goal. Because soccer felt like it was over for me, I realized how free I would be, time-wise—and how somehow my world, which had the potential to be so encompassing, had always centered mainly around soccer. And that's when it hit me—I didn't want to just replace that missing focus. I wanted to make it something really big, so big that it would challenge me and really mean something. At that moment, I decided to finish my first novel, something I had always wanted to do and could be remembered for. I ended up making my authorship and company my high school legacy.

When I achieved success and left that chapter of my legacy behind, I realized I had the chance to continue to develop. As many of us continue to move along our daily paths, we can get so caught up in details that we lose sight of the bigger picture. Remembering there is a bigger picture to life and not losing focus on it can make forging the path to success an almost instinctual daily routine. If you take anything from my short story, take these pointers:

1. **Money shouldn't be the close.** Don't make it your end goal. Yes, it can buy nice things, like cars or clothes, but even Tsar Nicholas II of Russia, one of the wealthiest monarchs ever, couldn't take any of his billions with him beyond the grave. Money is important, but view it as a step toward an end result.
2. **Follow what you're passionate about.** Don't be that person who goes for the job they hate and waits until it's too late to pursue the one they love. Your gut is a powerful tool—one day will pass by, then the next, until it's too late. Carpe diem!
3. **Be compassionate and kind.** I learned early on that winning over people's hearts with kindness creates a loyal and true respect—fear only alienates others while limiting your overall potential. At the end of the day, how you treated someone is what they'll remember.
4. **Trust in something greater than yourself.** Specific to each individual, this can be spirituality, religion, metaphysics, the universe and nature, or anything, really. The feeling that you are part of something unfathomably great will only inspire you to play your role with more life. Remember, legacies—no matter how prominent throughout history—are all tied together. Recognizing that, and using it to live and achieve not just for yourself but for everyone else, is only doing what's right.

So far, you have tackled the first step toward achieving success by learning to have an open mind, recognizing who you are and why you are so, and diving into the importance that each and every legacy has. Knowing that history is one of your most powerful tools, understand that by brainstorming on your own legacy, you are beginning to see what achievement(s) will not only result in success, but happiness, too. Your goal shouldn't be to choose just any legacy, but one that improves upon the past—a surefire way of thinking that will get you ahead of your global competition.

Chapter 3:
Doctor Who?

Now that you've read this far, I have a quick question I want you to ask yourself: what do you need to ascertain the historical significance of an event of legacy, or indeed whether the event or legacy ever actually existed? To put it another way, how can you truly take advantage of what you're able to get from events instead of just scraping the surface (something anyone can do)? The answer is through the use of general knowledge.

General knowledge is culturally valued information, and in this specific case I am referring to knowledge drawn from a variety of subjects, backgrounds, or experiences. As an example to the question above, imagine trying to discuss the effects and ethical significance of the Holocaust without knowing that the Holocaust took place, or perhaps without knowing World War II had occurred. The more you know, the easier it is for you to understand what you hear, read, and experience, as well as to learn new things. Obtaining and maintaining a broad field of knowledge is useful in many practical situations—jobs, interviews, dates, and intellectual conversation are only a few.

General knowledge not only contributes to your understanding of the world around you but as another plus, it is a personal enrichment that pours into your potential for success. Knowing that you need to have an open mind is only a preliminary step, of course—to actually open your mind and create an advantage when trying to achieve success, general knowledge is deeply important. People who know and understand are empowered to act and to make their own choices. People who do not know or understand become pawns in life, and they are acted upon.

The Power in Knowledge

Most people never really take the time to think about knowledge itself. In this case, I'm referring to the fact that there are two basic types of knowledge: general and specialized.

- **General knowledge** comprises information such as all kinds of events in history and their repercussions, how-to instructions, and surface-scraping concepts from a broad range of subjects. Example questions in the field of general knowledge: When was World War II fought? What is the universe basically made up of?

- **Specialized knowledge** is knowledge that pertains to a specific purpose (like your business or profession) and in-depth concepts from specific subjects. Example questions in the field of specialized knowledge: In which battle in World War II did the most Luftwaffe bombers raid a city? What elements make up proteins?

Both general and specialized knowledge are important in many ways. As we discussed earlier, general knowledge allows us to understand and analyze events, legacies, and the world around us. Over time, though, general knowledge can become useless, if not applied practically. Specialized knowledge is used to focus in on a subject—you can use this deeper kind of understanding to improve upon your skills and talents.

In combination, you can use general knowledge to see all the dots (opportunities) around you, and through specific knowledge, you can not only see how the dots connect but find new, unseen ways to improve upon those connections. Recognizing that time waits for no one and filling yourself with knowledge can be time consuming, and remembering these quick tips may help:

Make it a must to surround yourself with positive, intelligent, and driven individuals. Eventually, you can focus on surrounding yourself with a team of individuals who specialize in different areas of knowledge—this can help save time.

Know the difference between *intelligent*, *smart*, and *wise*. Intelligence is something you are born with. It is related to your ability to learn. On the other hand, how smart you are relates to learned inferences—when you study and learn, you can become smarter. Lastly, wisdom is the ability to use experiences and learned information in making good decisions, and the knowledge of your own capabilities and ethics.

Broadening Your Horizons

When I think back to what has given me such a huge advantage in the global community today, I realize that my interest in certain topics pushed me ahead of the competition. Below are a few of the subjects I recommend at least scraping the surface of—mainly because, from personal experience, they have helped me connect with a variety of people, improve on concepts or products through unique connections, think critically in different situations, develop as a person, and reach a higher level of success.

These subjects are also great avenues to purse at the very least as general knowledge if you need some ideas on where to start broadening your mental scope:

Technology and Computer Science
Computer science underlies most innovation today, from biotechnology to cinematography to national security. Technology not only includes computers, televisions, and cell phones, but equipment used on farms to help grow and maintain the food we eat, medical machines, and all other electronics.

Why study it: The ability to create and adapt new technologies distinguishes computer science as a field and its importance in today's society. Technology includes the invention of new, more effective medicines and enhanced machines in any industry or aspect of life. It comes in many forms, and all of these forms are important.

Philosophy
All humans engage in philosophy in one form or another, because we are innately philosophizing creatures. Philosophy is about gaining a better understanding of ourselves and our world—and since that is what humans naturally desire, humans quite readily engage in philosophical speculation and questioning.

Why study it: Anything that requires careful thinking, systematic reasoning, and an ability to ask and address difficult questions will benefit from your studying philosophy. Anyone who cares about whether or not their thinking is reasonable, well founded, well developed, and coherent should also look into this subject.

Metaphysics
Metaphysics is the branch of philosophy relating to the study of existence. It is the foundation of a worldview. It answers the question "What is?" It encompasses everything that exists, as well as the nature of existence itself. It explores whether the world is real or merely an illusion. It is a fundamental view of the world around us.

Why study it: Metaphysics is the foundation of philosophy. Without an explanation or an interpretation of the world around us, we would be helpless to deal with reality. We could not feed ourselves or act to preserve our lives. The degree to which our metaphysical worldview is correct is the degree to which we are able to comprehend the world and act accordingly. Without this firm foundation, all knowledge becomes suspect. Any flaw in our view of reality will make it more difficult to live.

Languages
Languages are part of a human system of communication that uses arbitrary signals, such as voice sounds, gestures, or written symbols. The study of language is called linguistics.

Why study it: Whether in writing, by phone, on the Internet, or in person, we all desire to be heard and understood and to be able to understand those around us. We use language to teach, to make our feelings known, and to read and enjoy books that interest us. Learning a second language also provides great advantages in life. People who speak more than one language think differently than those who don't. When you learn and speak another language, you become smarter, build multitasking skills, fence off Alzheimer's and dementia, improve your memory, and become more perceptive.

History

The word *history* is used in two senses. It can mean the record of events or events themselves. In a wider sense, history is all that has occurred—not merely all the phenomena of human life, but those of the natural world as well. It includes everything that undergoes change—therefore, the whole universe, and every part of it.

Why study it: History helps us understand other cultures and gives us a field full of human experience. By looking back at history, you can analyze other cultures, which contributes to understanding change. Change comes every day and all the time, and without knowledge of history, you don't have the background you need to prepare for the inevitable. History is also essential for determining what good citizenship is.

Business

Some would hold that a business is a solution for creating value among many people who voluntarily contribute time, risk, and resources with the intent of enriching themselves. It can include many aspects, like the exchange of goods or services, administration, finance, relationships, and more.

Why study it: The exchange of goods and services can benefit all. Consumers can obtain goods and services that they can't grow, raise, manufacture, or perform for themselves.

Literature

Literature helps us understand and make sense of the world around us. Through literature, we explore the human condition and analyze how people think and feel and why. We see the world through the eyes of different writers from different cultures and in turn learn the ways to deal with things happening around us.

Why study it: Literature enables us to develop our analytical skills and promotes open-mindedness. Without literature, we lack insight into and understanding of human nature.

Politics

A very basic definition of politics is the application of ethics to a group of people.

Why study it: Politics tells you how a society must be set up and how people should act within that society. Except for hermits, this comes up a lot.

Epistemology

Epistemology is the study of our method of acquiring knowledge. It answers the question, "How do we know?" It encompasses the nature of concepts, the constructing of concepts, the validity of the senses, and logical reasoning, as well as thoughts, ideas, memories, emotions, and all things mental.

Why study it: Epistemology is the explanation of how we think. It allows us to separate the true from the false by determining a proper method of evaluation. We need it in order to use and obtain knowledge of the world around us. Without epistemology, we could not think. More specifically, we would have no reason to believe our thinking was productive or correct, rather than being random images flashing through our minds. With an incorrect epistemology, we would not be able to distinguish truth from error. The consequences are obvious. The degree to which our epistemology is correct is the degree to which we understand reality, and the degree to which we can use that understanding to advance our lives and goals.

The Unspoken Advantage

"Knowledge is power" is a common phrase—but in reality, of course, knowledge is *potential* power. The question is, once you have that potential, how can you harness it to be successful? The answer is effective application. This means that every decision made, whether in the field of life or business, is informed by a clear understanding of its value, potential greater effect, and, in some cases, its nature.

A good personal example is in how I trained for my second black belt. After every important event or activity, I reviewed the experience to identify successes and failures to find ways to improve for the future. This is a process I use regularly in my own business ventures and social interactions. By looking back at the past to gain knowledge, I analyze the occurrence to come up with solutions for previous failures, so as to succeed the next time.

Essentially, the way to use knowledge is by applying it—especially in new ways. One person may not see a connection between politics and business, maybe because they don't like one or the other but most likely because they don't have enough knowledge on both of the subjects. You, on the other hand, know to look for normally unseen connections, like the fact that one definition of politics might be the practice of balancing and distributing power, and to do so, understanding relationships is key—something any successful man knows is important in business. Of course, that is not even looking at the connections between economics and politics.

This is an advantage you cannot pass by if you wish to truly be successful and achieve your goals in today's world of constant global competition, and it applies to almost any field. Remember, knowledge alone is only potential power—it's all about what you do with it and how you choose to apply it.

Chapter 4:
Anti-Procrastination

When the word "productivity" comes to mind, it may conjure images of people working long, hard days or constantly contributing to their specific job or goal. Or it may bring up images of entrepreneurship, a product being developed, or even some form of success. Bill Gates, for example, is clearly a very productive man—founder of Microsoft, global philanthropist, investor, author, not to mention the wealthiest person the planet as of April 2014. But despite its being one of the keys to success for any future achiever, many people don't understand the vital role of productivity, let alone how it works.

Procrastination is rampant, not just for the youth but in people of all ages. The formal definition of *productive* is "The quality, state, or fact of being able to generate, create, enhance, or bring forth goods and services." Productive people use their time and resources wisely, and their success can be measured in income and overall increased sales and growth.

I am frequently asked by other professionals and people struggling to balance a variety of projects, their goals, and procrastination, "How do you run several businesses, write multiple novels, meet deadlines, attend university, tour the country, walk your dog, and still have free time?" My answer is always "Through maximized productivity, efficiency, and time management." I have found from personal and other people's experience that a lack of understanding of productivity and procrastination results in personal-life issues, lack of sleep, and smaller negative results. In many cases, all that is required is an understanding of what productivity is based on and methods of how to enhance it.

The Zone

Imagine for a second that you are running in a race. You're completely focused on your body's movements; you can feel each muscle as power surges through it, the deep force of your lungs, and the firm earth beneath your feet. Time doesn't seem to exist, nor fatigue, and you can only see the finish line—you are in the zone.

This constantly debated phenomenon is commonly referred to as being "in the zone" (in athletics), "living in the moment," or just "flow." It's a mental state in which time flies, complete immersion the activity occurs, and every thought, action, and movement follows cohesively after the one before, in perfect harmony. Generally, the state is accompanied by a few factors, some of which can be:

1. A clear, challenging, and reachable goal

2. Complete focus, concentration, and attention
3. A loss of feeling of "the self"
4. Lack of awareness of physical needs
5. Complete immersion in the activity at hand
6. A feeling of timelessness

Although this super-productive state is a supreme advantage to anyone, many people don't know what causes it—or how to enter it. The simplest guide to live by for achieving flow is to meet at least these requirements:

- Energy (don't be tired, be full of life)
- Focus (be ready to act with a specific goal in mind)
- No distractions (even the slightest can disrupt gradual flow)
- Music (not for all people, but it can help increase productivity)

Also, laying out a plan of action (for certain activities) allows you to remain focused, and make sure you're passionate about something that directly relates to the activity. Remember, flow not only makes activities more enjoyable, but also aids in learning or improving skills, overall performance, and creativity in any activity.

Strength in Habits

The age-old search for a way to be more productive has led many to a misconception of what productivity is—and that is efficiency in "doing." Productivity is more than just doing more and doing it more quickly; it's about doing more with less. One of the biggest keys to being productive is commonly overlooked, because people don't see the huge potential advantage it holds, and that is habit. Habits contain great power for you to use on your path to success. Have you ever set out with the goal of doing something new and different, consistently? Habits come into play here. Habits can be extremely useful when utilized correctly, or detrimental when not.

Habits automate most routine tasks and free our minds up to engage with the world and preform on more complicated types of activities. For example, the average person does not have to think about talking, eating, or having to breathe. We can think as we walk or run because of the automated system our mind has. This automated system of habit reduces the amount our brain has to process, leaving the energy for other activities; in short, habitual actions require less physical and mental energy. But like most powerful tools, this has its negatives and positives—also known as good and bad habits.

The human brain is always looking for life patterns to form habits, but sadly the subconscious does not distinguish between what good habits and bad. Positive habits not only produce order and routine, but boost overall efficiency. Negative habits do the opposite—and in some cases can be physically or mentally damaging, like smoking, false commitment, and overeating. Understand that your strong habits are your strengths, just as your weak habits are your weaknesses. If you can understand what good and bad habits generally are, what current habits have positive and negative effects on you, and how to form new, better habits, you can control your productivity strength.

Here are some basic, general good habits to note and some bad ones to look out for:

Positive	Negative
Creating a system	Being trapped by false limits
Stopping multitasking	Working in a disruptive setting
Tackling your challenging tasks before lunch	Taking discouragement from other people
Having a specific time to focus on yourself	Creating and evaluating at the same time
Taking more, quicker breaks	Always researching, never "doing"

The question is, how do you gain control of your productivity strength? The rest of this chapter divulges what to start with, why, and how to do it.

Mental Attitude

One of the most obvious differences between those who succeed and fail in life or in achieving their goals is mentality. Everyone starts out as a beginner. But the dropouts on the path to success give up at the first sign of adversity, and the amateurs achieve to some extent, only to become complacent and sometimes lose their will to improve. Those who truly succeed look toward constant improvement, and not just in one specific aspect of life. What gets those who succeed to the finish line is derived from one type of mental attitude: constant improvement.

Can't just doesn't exist in the minds of those who will succeed. There is always a way, even when all may seem lost—and you have the ability and skill to find it. Nor is it just that you can, but rather that you will (and there is no way you won't) achieve to reach your goals. That is the mentality a truly successful person had, has, and will continue to have—just as you either already do or will learn to. The path to your success doesn't end at a predetermined point, but only when you choose to stop journeying on it. Talent comes into play often when measuring success, but talent is only latent potential—something your mentality directly influences the use of. If we choose to believe a person's talent is fixed, including our own, we are cutting off any chances for growth. By believing that talent or any ability develops based on hard work, we open ourselves to limitless opportunities.

The reality is some people are born with natural talents, and sometimes they are even referred to as geniuses. Some believe that when a person with greater natural talent works hard, those with less can't compete. **Throw out that misconception**—for if you believe it, you only create a habit of mental doubt. Remember, anyone can be a genius of hard work; it just takes, well, hard work. Below are a few ways that having a positive mental attitude can help you succeed:

1. **Improves time management skills** (a positive attitude allows for easier focus)
2. **Attracts support systems** (by staying positive, you spread cooperation as others feel your positive attitude; nobody likes complainers)
3. **Pushes creativity boosts** (a positive mentality keeps your mind open—which improves the quality of your knowledge)
4. **Reduces stress levels** (some stress may be good for a short goal, but longer goals require you to be healthy mentally and physically)
5. **Increases proactivity** (your mentality will push you to improve—you can work to solve issues before rather than after they arise)

Don't confuse having a positive attitude or mentality with being a Pollyanna. Being positive shouldn't keep you from identifying problems, but rather should push you to identify and solve them through your proactive efforts. Lastly, try to distinguish between what you think of as work and play. For example, when I write and have a deadline, I don't think or call having to write work—because if I do, I get stressed, and quality suffers. Because I absolutely love to write and have fun doing it, I think of it as play—even if it is for work.

Inspiring Environment

Motivation and mentality work best in an environment that supports your goals. If your environment is not conducive to achieving your goals, you will spend more energy and willpower trying to succeed, resulting in less productivity. Imagine trying to eat healthy for a couple of weeks straight when your home is filled with fatty food, you eat fast food regularly, and you buy sweets on impulse. Meeting the challenge for a day or two may be possible, but eventually your motivation to fight your environment will probably run dry.

When you start utilizing energy that is usually spent working against a negative environment, you're more likely to effectively take action toward your goal, consistently. This applies to performance, time management, earning more money, and many other goals. As an example, when I wrote my first novel in high school, I made sure to form an environment that supported working toward my goal of writing every other day. I went and purchased a ton of mechanical pencils and pens and two notebooks, each a different size, to make sure I left myself no excuse not to write. I set a specific time when I knew I wouldn't be disturbed and printed out the answers to any strategic writing questions I thought I could have. I told people I was making way with my novel, to push myself to honor my word. I even posted chapters online to get feedback and interactions about it.

All of those actions ensured my environment only helped support what I wanted to do—and because of them, I finished the manuscript in seven months (with, of course, a couple of extended school breaks here and there). Even when an environment is already positively affecting productivity, there is always room to improve on it. There are many different types of environments you can try changing up, like:

> ➤ Physical environments: Your room, home, office, workplace, or any place you can go, like a café or library
> ➤ Communities: Online, offline, and people you socialize with
> ➤ Technology: Your computer or tablet (desktop, browser, system setup) and your phone (smartphone)

Just by trying to do the same activity in a different environment, you can see the difference in productivity management. But how can you create a more productive environment? Here are some methods:

A. An existing environment: Look around your workspace right now. Does it motivate you? Inspire you? Is it full of distractions? Many people don't realize that they are working against their environments or in places that feel like "can't work here" settings. Instead of fighting it, change it up. By turning off the telly, moving that distracting book you want to get back to, and logging out of social media, you allow a sense of clarity in your workplace. Even adding a poster or piece of art by or of someone or something you admire may give you inspiration.

B. Finding a new environment: Have you ever hung out, watched television, read, and maybe even slept in the same room before? Maybe you even work in one room or office and take breaks from work there too. Try separating spaces—working in one specific room or area and breaking in an entirely different one. Environmental habits form quite easily over time, especially negative ones. How can you expect to tell yourself to work in an area that you also use to sleep, or hang out and socialize in? By splitting up environments based on activity type, you form mental habits—when you're sitting on the couch, it's relaxing time, while your mind knows that when you sit down in the study, you're there to work. Again, make sure these settings are arranged to support your desired goal.

By using your environment strategically, you can increase productivity as you try to achieve your goals more seamlessly.

M. D. O.

This acronym stands for music, diet, and online (the Internet), three of the biggest productivity-related concepts I get asked about while touring. A multitude of people seem to struggle with using M. D. O. in a way that benefits them, usually just because of a lack of understanding (common theme, eh?). Since ancient times, the varying positive qualities of music have spread from culture to culture. It isn't until relatively recently that the Internet and diet control have come into the light in terms of how they can positively and negatively effect productivity.

Music
Some music can provide an escape from reality, but at the very least, it can replace a disruptive and noisy environment with inspiring sounds. Picture yourself sitting in a library, and the table next to you is filled with a loud group of kids. I'm sure that the earphones on your table are looking very appealing right about now—how about popping them in and jamming to some tunes? Melodious sounds have been noted to release the biological chemical dopamine, improving a person's mood. Even so, music's effect on productivity seems to differ from person to person. Some people find that it inspires them and keeps them in the moment (something that can help instigate flow), while others find it doesn't help or is distracting. Personally, I like to listen to classical music, orchestral video game pieces, and movie scores when I work—but it all depends on you.

Diet
Controlling this allows you to influence your performance. This is because what you eat fuels your brain. Most of what you eat is broken down into glucose. Glucose is what keeps our brains awake and attentive. But what we have control over is not glucose itself, but the release of it in our bodies. For example, when you eat a piece of cake, glucose is released rapidly, and you can have about twenty minutes of attentive alertness. Then, your glucose level drops quickly, and you are left inattentive and less aware. If you were to eat oatmeal, your body would take longer to release glucose into your system. This results in having an extended period of higher glucose levels, allowing for better attentiveness and focus. Of course, there are quite a few more factors to the system, including your leptin levels (which regulate feeling full), but that is not for the here and now.

Essentially, the quality of food you choose to eat, not just the amount, does matter. Find foods that give your brain the steadiest fuel, like nuts, fish, and dark chocolate (as recommended by the W. H. O.). Trust me, working on an empty stomach amounts to nothing when compared to work done on a healthy, full one.

Online
Online and *offline* are common words in a variety of phrases in today's culture. I have found that the amount of time far too many people spend on websites like Facebook, Twitter, LinkedIn, Instagram, Imgur, and other popular social media sites, as well as just pointlessly surfing the web, is troubling. Negative effects include:

- No face-to-face communication
- Sexual exploitation
- Loss of privacy
- Addiction

- Insomnia
- Cyber bullying
- Limited physical activity
- Procrastination

But the Internet's positive features have far outweighed the negatives, for now, on an irrefutable global scale. And indeed, there are ways to use the online world to promote good habits and productivity. Here are a few tips to help with being productive while online:

1. Learn to type quickly
2. Keep social media on a separate browser
3. Find one of the many free programs that limit usage of certain websites by day
4. Carve out time to stay organized by utilizing what you have learned so far in this book; productivity optimization should be far easier

Exercise

List some of the general habits you have now and some that you wish to replace or improve upon below:

PART TWO

Chapter 5:
The Question

So far, we have focused on opening your mind, a variety of tools and methods that contribute to success, and a guide toward achieving your goals successfully. But one of the most important methods I and many other successful people have use and continue to use to achieve and reach new heights is *innovation*. I say "method" because innovating, which has already been a running theme throughout this book, is a process. I call it the Inno-Process. The skill to innovate will give you the capability to succeed in any aspect of life or business, or at the very least will greatly improve your chances of success.

Understanding what innovation is and what innovators do is essential; innovation is the hallmark of success all around us, like in the case of Apple products (Steve Jobs) and the invention of email (Shiva Ayyadurai). Having a process of innovation to apply to your own life is an immeasurable advantage against the global competition that faces you today, and the next few chapters attempt to give you just that. In many cases, the core of sustainability is innovation—so naturally you want to start the process by creating a massive amount of ideas, right? Well, no. Ideas are of course the seed of innovation, but knowing how to produce useful, relevant seeds is just as important as the seeds themselves. How do you start? By asking questions—more specifically, by asking the *right* questions.

Questioning Your World

Questions are slot containers in your mind where answers fit. Without the question, the answer has nowhere to land. With no slot, the answers just wisp past us. You have to have the will to know—to ask the question that reveals that latent container that the answer fits in. Here are a few types of questions:

- Factual: Asking based on obvious facts or awareness. Usually, answers are either right or wrong. Example question: According to Steve Jobs's biography, *Steve Jobs,* was Jobs born on an island?
- Divergent: Questions that allow for exploration of different variations or scenarios. Answers to these questions are usually less clear cut. Example question: In the relationship between Jobs and Wozniak, what would have happened if they hadn't worked together on the Atari project in 1973?
- Harmonious: Asking based on material that is presented, known, or read. Answers tend to be more objective than subjective. Example question: Reflecting on *Steve Jobs,* what influence did Jobs's brief time in college have on his eventual success?

The Question

- Interpretative: Questions that often require sophisticated and deep thinking. Answers frequently derive from comparing or contrasting a variety of different perspectives to form conclusions. Example question: Compare and contrast the Steve Jobs's path to success and J. K. Rowling's.

Your mind grows by asking questions. To drive innovation, there are some basic ones you can start asking, like:

1. What can I look at in a new way?
2. What can I connect in a new way?
3. What could I use in a new way?
4. How could I use space and time to recontextualize?
5. How can I look at ---- in a new way?
6. How can I connect ---- with ---- in a new way, or connect ---- with a new concept?
7. How can I use ---- in a new way?
8. What could I create that would be authentically new?

Exercise

Use the basic questions above to come up with some personal examples. Write a few down below. Don't include any resource limitations like finances or current knowledge.

When I was seventeen, I asked myself a very specific question on my path to achieving success: "How can I make money with the skills I have at no current cost to myself?" I eventually modified this question to "How can I make money with the skills I have, at no current cost to myself, in a way that is and will continue to be in demand?" Although fairly simple on its face, this parent question paved the way to questions like "What skills cost me nothing?" and "What products or services are in demand and will continue to be in the future?" The best example of my process from the list above was question #6, but my version fed the Inno-Process question through the resource limitations I had at that time.

When you have a specific goal you're trying to achieve and you have limitations like lack of resources or funding, setting limits on the Inno-Process questions can be the best way to start. As in my teenage story, my original goal at the time was simple: I wanted to find a way to make some extra money while in high school. I took that goal and rewrote it in question form, producing THE question from which my Inno-Process began. I asked myself the right questions with no limitations on them, only to have to move on to the next step—finding the inspiration to produce new answers to those questions.

Chapter 6:
The Muses

In today's culture, we tend to look at ability and potential final results while overlooking the vital role of inspiration in success. Inspiration opens us to new possibilities—possibilities that allow us to transcend our current life status and limitations to move into something greater. Inspiration isn't easy to manipulate, as one may expect something that can transform apathy to empathy so that the previously unseen can be seen and utilized would be. When a person is inspired, they attempt more and can climb to greater heights, a step in the building process that can determine levels of success and failure.

Throughout the ages, successful and timeless people like John Milton, Pablo Picasso, and Steve Jobs have utilized the idea of the Muses: the deified versions of human inspiration and talent. In ancient Greece, people would call on the Muses for inspiration to feed their talents in any of the nine subjects they represented (history, music, comedy, drama, dance, singing, poetry, astronomy, and epics). The Muses represented not only inspiration but also what was most valued in their culture. Of course, you don't have to believe in the Muses as the ancient Greeks did to recognize the importance they represented, and even though still some think that their divine treatment had negative effects, history has proven elsewise. Now, it's your turn.

The Musemobile

Some people get inspired to achieve by a beautiful piece of art, soul-touching music, or even by nature itself. Any one of us can be creative in our own way, but everyone is different, and so is what can inspire us. Finding what inspires you is a necessary step on the road to success, and here are a few methods to try:

1. Don't follow the obvious route. If you take the same route to work every day, try an alternative one if time permits—by challenging what you're used to, you open your mind to the new. When you see something new after seeing the same thing day after day, you focus in on it, and that allows for new possibilities.
2. Schedule Muse sessions. I don't mean trying to call the gods of ancient Greek mythology down into your living space—what this means is finding time to expose yourself to creativity. This can be by viewing art, listening to music, reading a great story, being around interesting people, or anything similar.

Personally, I find inspiration in a multitude of ways: walking on the beach, gazing at the stars, jogging with my dog, or just listening to soundtracks from my favorite movies or shows.

The Success Initiative

Exercise
If you currently know what inspires you, describe it and how it affects you in the space below. If you don't, jot down some ideas of things that you think may inspire you, such as seeing a good movie. Trying different activities is the best way to find what inspires you.

Remember, define your end goal and rewrite it in question form, so that you have THE (parent) question. Then, find and draw on your inspiration, so that you can transcend to see the possibilities that hold the answers you need to achieve success.

Chapter 7:
Imagination

A reel within our own minds that allows us to see, and in some cases experience, what may or may not be or what doesn't currently exist—that is the imagination. People throw the word around quite commonly, for example, saying things like "That person has a brilliant imagination." It is also frequently used to describe mental imagery, picturing something in your mind. In most cultures and civilizations, writers, musicians, and artists are looked upon as having the greatest imaginations. When I wrote *Zephyr the West Wind*, I had to create a world, characters, events, and plots and continue to develop them—I couldn't have done so without inspiration or imagination.

The imagination is used throughout a variety of industries, including business. To answer THE question(s) in your first step toward innovation, you must find inspiration to fuel your imagination to form ideas. In 2013, I wanted to develop a better system of communication between one of my company's division's clients and staff. I brought every assistant- and secretarial-position staff member together to discuss how we could improve our customer service. At the meeting, I asked, "How can we be more efficient with our customer communication, leaving them not just happier but also inclined to return?"

I then split the staff into groups, instructing them to devise a variety of different scenarios (like interacting with clients from different regions of the world) and ways to use them to our advantage. At first, we had a bit of a challenge releasing their imaginations, so I tried an exercise to get their creativity fired up; I took the lip balm I had in my pocket and said, "Give me ways this relates to our company." After many shots of imagination-charged ideas, we returned to the original issue, this time coming up with out-of-the-box ways to improve. Imagination can be used not only to visualize new ideas but also to conceptualize the design, production, and marketing of existing ones.

Stigma

Ancient Greeks aside, more recently, imaginative people and concepts frequently have a social stigma attached to them. As children usually have vivid and untamed imaginations, adults often feel like they have to prove their maturity or practicality to others or themselves. They attach a connotation of immaturity to imagination and specifically fantasy, the epitome of a wild imagination; a person can feel grown up by simply proclaiming that "fantasy is just that—not real, so it doesn't matter," or that "reality is what matters most."

The Success Initiative

　　　　　Everyone has their own likes and dislikes; this isn't about liking fantasy-related subjects or materials, like novels or TV shows of the genre, but rather being able to appreciate imagination and creative ideas by understanding their relevance to reality and the improvement of it. Having read the previous chapters, you should understand the value of imagination and creativity to society and to your success—because you know that when you have an open mind, you also gain better access to the limitless possibilities for success around you. Imagination isn't a weakness or a sign of immaturity, but rather the ability of the revolutionaries—those who have the potential to affect the world.

The First Wave

In the Inno-Process, imagination is what you use to come up with the first draft of your answers to THE question(s). For example, when you've put your goal into the form of a question, like "How can I use my cooking skills to make money?", you would want to note any and all ideas that may apply to answering THE question, whether they seem possible or not.

Exercise
Below, write down ideas that answer one of your own questions (which should already be in the format of the eight question types from Chapter 5). To continue our example above, answers might include "I would found a one-man cooking business" or "I would produce cooking recipe books." Remember: let your imagination run free when answering!

Chapter 8:
Enlightenment

Innovative breakthroughs occur when a person disrupts prevailing ideas of reality and, in most cases, improves upon them. Using our imaginations is a step toward making that happen, but there are two "gates" of creativity in the Inno-Process. Each gate leaves us with what I refer to as drafts. The last chapter focused on the first gate, where you let your imagination run free to produce answers and solutions. The second gate requires a greater touch of present reality—the creation of answers, solutions, or a plan realistically based on the present.

Evaluation

By taking the ideas you come up with in the first gate of imagination and evaluating them based on a few defined guidelines, you can use your ideas right away to try to achieve the answers your imagination came up with. For example, imagine that you are a college student with very little to spend on what isn't necessary for school and to live. THE question you came up with was "How can I make money with my cooking skills?", and your first imagined answer was "By founding my own restaurant." Even if your goal is to found a restaurant eventually, you need to make headway toward that goal, and in order to do so, you must use the current reality that applies to you.

As that college student and assuming your cooking skills are genuinely brilliant, you would proceed to asking questions like "How could I found a restaurant with almost no money?" or the more in-depth "As I'm in college, is there a step I can take now toward achieving my goal?" For now, we will rule out the option of dropping out—for the sake of the example and because of the importance of both general and specific knowledge. These questions provide ways to set up a realistic plan to achieve your end goal by establishing parameters to stay on a realistic track. In other words, use the reality of your life.

Parameters

With a currently unrealistic method to solve the college student's goal, the next step is to set up a plan that can be put into action as immediately as possible. By applying the parameters of not having enough money and currently being in college to the idea of founding a restaurant to make money with your cooking skills, you bring your idea to the very limit of reality—by applying the imagined idea to what is currently possible. Parameters are important not just because an idea like "building a flying car" may not apparently be possible based on technological limitations, but also because many people don't have a huge amount of resources (like money or time).

By defining parameters based on your current limits, you can set up a possible route toward starting to achieve your goal, even when held back by such limits. In the area below, take an "out of this world" goal, like "building a teleportation pad," that is relevant to you.

Exercise

Write down some parameters based on what is or may be holding you back, like lack of resources or current knowledge, below:

Enlightenment

Guided Imagination

By understanding the use of parameters and how to create them by evaluation of your current limitations, you can determine which of your imagined concepts or routes lead to dead ends. This saves you time, because you don't have to try as many routes before finding out your goal as it stands isn't achievable, and you can use each and every dead end to propel you forward. Don't regard them as failures. If you can't do "y," note that if you can imagine it, there may be a route to return to later on to accomplish it—we'll discuss this in Chapter 9.

With a defined goal, you have asked THE question(s). You have found your inspiration and fueled your imagination to produce extraordinary first-draft answers. Now, turn to evaluate those first drafts so that you can develop a second draft—which will lead to an achievable, innovative, solution-based action plan.

Chapter 9:
Innovation

From Chapter 5, each step has been a building block—blocks that when used together can make achieving a goal or dream a reality. After evaluating your first-draft answer(s) and creating second-draft ones based on reality-defined parameters, you should have the necessary information to formulate a step-by-step plan to achieve the original goal that THE question derived from.

Let's go back to the college student cook example. In the first step, we took the goal of wanting to make money through cooking and made it into THE question: How can I use cooking to make money? In the second and third steps, we would have found inspiration to fuel our imagination to come up with unpolished answers. In the fourth step, we used current limitations based on our personal reality to set parameters, so that we could evaluate and develop our raw imaginative answers based on those parameters.

A final-draft answer in this case might be "founding a college campus personal cook business," based on the facts that the student needs to be around the college and has no money. The latter part would be solved by having the clients pay for the food and supplies while providing the student with a place to cook.

The Forged Path

With a goal that can be carried out (let's say immediately), the next question is where to start, now that you have your answer(s). To begin implementation, you need an action plan. Some people naturally use the steps above to come up with fantastic ideas, but they often fail because they don't come up with a plan that pushes them through to success. By having followed this process, you should have everything you need for the plan's structure already.

Begin by drawing a timeline and writing down your second-draft goal at one end. Because this is your revised answer to your version of THE question, you need a way of achieving it. This will require different steps depending on what your goal is. The other end of your timeline should start with the first action you must take to reach the end—for some, that may be research on a topic, going to the store to buy a pencil and pen, contacting a fellow employee, or a variety of other possible first steps.

Below, I have included a very basic example, based on the college cook, on what an action plan should start looking like. It includes a measurement of progress (defined deadlines), any investment costs, time, and additional resources.

Action Plan Example:

Name: Don Cook

Date: --/--/----

Raw Goal: To use cooking to make money.

Step #	Date	Description
Step 1	02/14	Check availability of starting campus service
Step 2	02/15	Research starting a business
Step 3	02/07	Name business or organization
Step 4	--/--	Another later step would be listed here
Step 5	--/--	Another later step would be listed here
Step 6	03/11	Research marketing
Step 7	--/--	Another later step would be listed here
Step 8	04/13	Find and enroll clients
Step 9	05/19	Open business and start servicing

End Result: College campus personal cook business/service

As far as being revolutionary, the final result in the example above may not be top tier—but the structure and process should work for almost any success-achievement plan. The gold isn't the brilliant innovative idea at the end of the timeline, but the steps taken to achieve and accomplish such a feat. Remember, your action timeline should end with an achievable result. If you don't have "y" at the beginning but need "y" to achieve Step 7, some of the steps before Step 7 should result in you obtaining "y." I suggest having that result be a shorter-term goal first, so that if you have a longer project in mind, the short-term list can build up to the longer one.

With your goal in mind and a path leading through your journey ahead to achieve it, you must make sure one last time that you are prepared and ready for the challenging adventure ahead.

The Abyss of Fear

We are programmed to survive, right down to our genes. One of the ways our subconscious follows this programming is by usually believing the least-risky course to be the best. Risk invites the possibility of failure—especially if the risk is extremely high, or you don't deem yourself ready to take it. Of course, this can be manifested in a variety of different ways, a common one being fear.

Children are prime examples; many fear the dark, and their imaginations can go wild when thinking of what could be lurking. But the shadows represent something we can't control—the unknown. Although they probably wouldn't admit it because of the social stigma associated with it, many people never get over their childhood fear of the dark. But, for this book, our focus is on a certain fear that can hold many people back without realizing it: the fear of success. It may sound counterintuitive, as most people probably wouldn't say "I would not like to succeed," but an important point people often forget or don't realize is that being programmed for survival isn't the same as being tuned for success.

Think about it—survival is low risk, but most dreams, aspirations, and big goals carry big risks; at least, that's how your subconscious is likely to interpret it. Achievement of success means change, and change equates to the unknown—something we naturally fear. To survive, fear of the unknown is a parameter, and so the subconscious tries to avoid the shadows. You never know, a hydra may be hiding in that lake you're about to pass by!

In reality, by avoiding the unknown, you stay in your comfort zone. When you're achieving your goal, you sometimes can't see everything around you, and survival is often easier when you can. Fear often manifests in certain ways; commonly, people who try to make change and can't seem to are engaging in self-sabotage without realizing it. Here are some examples that may sound familiar:

- Procrastination: Putting off work, projects, or assignments by finding ways to distract yourself with unnecessary activities. A common one I see now is Facebook, or surfing the web.
- All bark, no bite: Always talking about your dreams and goals, only to spend your time watching television or hanging out on the Internet or social media rather than taking steps to achieve what you talk about.
- Negative self-talk: By looking at life negatively, you sabotage yourself with thoughts like "What's the point of applying? I won't get in anyway." This goes against the mental attitude in Chapter 4.

The simplest key is to believe in your ability to adapt to change and to set up a step-by-step process to achieve success. Include in it ways of eliminating self-sabotaging behavior. An example could be getting rid of cable in your home for a month, or going to a place without Internet access when you don't need the web for work.

Fear isn't an enemy of success. If you see failure as a necessary step toward achieving your goals, it becomes part of your path to success instead of a dead end on it. Remember, the only thing you have to fear in life is missing out!

Alibis

People who are able to achieve their goals have a sufficient amount of confidence, courage, commitment, and vision, all of which are developed over time and through effort. Can anyone develop these qualities? The answer: yes, anyone and everyone can. The real question is, why don't they? Why do so many people continue to imagine or talk about their dreams, but not create them for themselves?

Well, it's because they make excuses. In many cases, they allow fear to emerge as excuses, their ways of avoiding the risk. Here are three common ones to look out for so that you can catch yourself in the act:

1. **I don't have the money.** This shouldn't be a problem after reading the previous chapters of this book. Review the Inno-Process if needed, for there is always a way to achieve.
2. **What if it doesn't work?** Every failure should be used as a step to get closer to success.
3. **This is just me, I can't change it.** Anything you think and feel can be changed—as long as you recognize this, you can begin to change your own life.

Packing Up

By now, I'm sure you have realized that success is reached through a series of steps, and that you can create your own path to achieve it, no matter what your background, age, or status. Everyone's path is different—some are short and easy, while others are long and filled with great turmoil. Nevertheless, you know that you have what it takes to beat every challenge that stands in your way, and that each one is only there to make you stronger.

I suggest reviewing the earlier chapters of this book every once in a while to refresh your understanding of yourself, the world around you, and the power you possess to make your dreams come true.

Chapter 10:
The Will of Fire

Usually only noticeable in dire moments, humans have the amazing ability to fight against all odds—and often come out on top. This ability is based on what I call the Will of Fire. It represents your drive not just to live, but to succeed—to live to the best of your ability. This flame, on an individual level and globally (all of humanity), is something we are all part of. We can't escape it.

Lighting the Torch

One of our jobs as part of the human race is to help humanity's flame burn continuously stronger. To do so, your own will must be burning strongly, so that you can light flames that may be burning low in others. When you succeed, or are on your path to success, use your own achievements to inspire others to do the same. By doing so, you aren't just benefiting yourself, but all of humanity. The more you fight to make your dreams a reality, the brighter your flame shines. If you use your eventual success not merely to achieve your own goals but to aid others in achieving theirs by inspiring them, you will find yourself far happier in life.

Before we part, I also want to express the importance of general charity. Whether through volunteering for food banks, charitable runs and events, or a private donation of any amount of time or money, every action counts. It doesn't have to be a financial gift; even just a small piece of your time does more wonders than many people realize. Charity is a great way to contribute to making the world a better place—and supporting humanity's Will of Fire.

You can achieve success while helping others along the way. It just requires a bit of compassion, and maybe even creativity.

In everything I do, from writing books to doing business, one of my intents is to always help make the world a better place in the best way I can—by helping others recognize they can achieve their dreams and make positive change as well. It has been an honor to meet you at this point on your path to success and happiness. I hope that my fire has helped your Will of Fire burn stronger through this book. As it is about time I say goodbye, I leave this last passage with you:

Recognize and never forget
We are all in this together
True strength doesn't stem from you alone,
But from the fire of all legacies
Past, present, and future

There are many realities
And even more dreams
But they all share the same wish

Now step forward
For your own path of choices lies ahead
To realize this wish
And make your dreams come true

About
R.J. Tolson

With five months left at age 17, Tolson spoke six languages (English, Spanish, Greek, Korean, Chinese, and Japanese), had finished his first novel, and had founded future web design division RJTINC. During his 18th year, Tolson founded multidivisional international company RJTIO, published *Zephyr the West Wina*, and began attending Whittier College (President Nixon's and Edwin Keh's alma mater). Comprising web division RJTINC (with 20 staff members), business consulting, and tutoring division R.L. Infinity Int., and internationally known Forever Trust Charity, RJTIO expanded into international business.

By age 19, Tolson was a multidivisional CEO managing over 50 contracted employees at RJTIO offices and outposts around the world, an award-winning author, a teacher of metaphysics, and a teenage philanthropist.

Now 20 years old, Tolson, managing over 100 contracted RJTIO employees and over 250,000 FT volunteers, featured on multiple national/international networks (NBC, ABC, CBS, Fox, Telemundo), has become an internationally recognized CEO and fantasy author of the Chaos Chronicles Series, founder of the Project: Limitless initiative, and author of the Project: Limitless book series. Tolson still teaches metaphysics and pursues innovation.

Tolson tours nationally and internationally on a literary campaign to promote reading and writing, along with entrepreneurship and the theme of innovation. This has included schools all over New England, Florida, Washington D.C., and China on an educational business trip, experiencing the culture meeting with fortune companies and executives. He has been a featured panelist at multiple festivals, including the Baltimore and Miami book festivals and the Virginia Festival of the Books.

Tolson attended and graduated from a private boarding high school, Cheshire Academy, and studies at Whittier College in California, where he currently lives. Aside from his writing skills, he also composes both classical and jazz music and produces pop and hip-hop music. He has trained in several martial arts and has a black belt in each.

Find more:
www.rjtolson.com

Follow:
Twitter: @RJTolson
Facebook: AuthorRJTolson
Instagram: RJTolson
Goodreads: RJ Tolson

www.ingramcontent.com/pod-product-compliance
Lightning Source LLC
Chambersburg PA
CBHW072016060426
42446CB00043B/2573